MACDONALD STARTERS

Post

Macdonald Educational

About Macdonald Starters

Macdonald Starters are vocabulary controlled information books for young children. More than ninety per cent of the words in the text will be in the reading vocabulary of the vast majority of young readers. Word and sentence length have also been carefully controlled.

Key new words associated with the topic of each book are repeated with picture explanations in the Starters dictionary at the end. The dictionary can also be used as an index for teaching children to look things up.

Teachers and experts have been consulted on the content and accuracy of the books.

Illustrated by : William Robertshaw

Editors : Peter Usborne, Su Swallow, Jennifer Vaughan

Reading consultant : Donald Moyle, author of *The Teaching of Reading* and senior lecturer in education at Edge Hill College of Education

Chairman, teacher advisory panel : F. F. Blackwell, general inspector for schools, London Borough of Croydon, with responsibility for primary education

Teacher panel : Elizabeth Wray, Loveday Harmer, Lynda Snowdon, Joy West

© Macdonald and Company (Publishers) Limited 1972
Third Impression 1974
Made and printed in Great Britain by Purnell & Sons Limited Paulton, Somerset

ISBN 0 356 03996 x
First published 1972 by Macdonald Educational
St Giles House
49-50 Poland Street
London W1

Some letters have come.
The postman brought them.
There is a letter for me.

1

When people send letters
they post them in a letter box.
2

A postman collects the letters
from the letter box.

3

The postman takes the letters
to the sorting office.
4

The postmen sort the letters.
They put the letters into bags.
The bags are called mail bags.

All these mail bags
are going to the same town.
Men put the mail bags
on to the train.

6

The fast train travels all night.
Postmen work inside the train.
Soon the train reaches the town.

Some letters must go a long way.
Aeroplanes carry them
across the world.
8

Sometimes ships carry letters.
Ships travel slowly.
The letters take a long time.

This man sends
lots of letters.
The woman types his letters.
10

Long ago,
people wrote with quills.
Quills were pens
made out of feathers.

11

Once there was no paper.
People wrote on soft clay.
They dried the clay in the sun.
12

Later, people used parchment.
Parchment was like paper.
It was made from animal skin.

13

Before there were any postmen,
messengers carried the letters.

14

People put seals on the letters.
The seal kept the letter closed.
You had to break the seal
to open the letter.

This is a mail coach.
It carried letters.
The man at the back blew a horn.
People knew the coach was coming.
16

Sometimes robbers
stopped a mail coach.
These robbers were called
highwaymen.

People paid for the letters
when they arrived.
Sometimes a person could not pay.
He could not have his letter.

18

This man invented stamps.
The first stamp was black.
It cost one old penny.
It was called a Penny Black.

Most countries have stamps now.
Here are some stamps
from all over the world.

20

There are not many stamps
like these.
People pay a lot of money for them.

See for yourself
See how many different stamps
you can collect.

22

Starter's **Post** words

letter
(page 1)

train
(page 6)

postman
(page 1)

aeroplane
(page 8)

sorting
office
(page 4)

world
(page 8)

mail bag
(page 5)

ship
(page 9)

23

type
(page 10)

clay
(page 12)

quill
(page 11)

parchment
(page 13)

pen
(page 11)

animal
(page 13)

write
(page 11)

messenger
(page 14)

seal
(page 15)

robber
(page 17)

mail
coach
(page 16)

stamp
(page 19)

blew
(page 16)

Penny
Black
(page 19)

horn
(page 16)

money
(page 21)